To

From

Flavia.

Beyond The Clouds
copyright © 1993 by Flavia Weedn
All rights reserved. Printed in Hong Kong.

For information write Andrews and McMeel,
a Universal Press Syndicate Company,
4900 Main Street, Kansas City, Missouri 64112

ISBN: 0-8362-4703-5

BEYOND
THE CLOUDS

Written and Illustrated
by Flavia Weedn

The

silent

tears of

the heart

hurt

the

most.

And

sometimes

it seems

as though

the hurt will

never go away.

But

every joy

in life

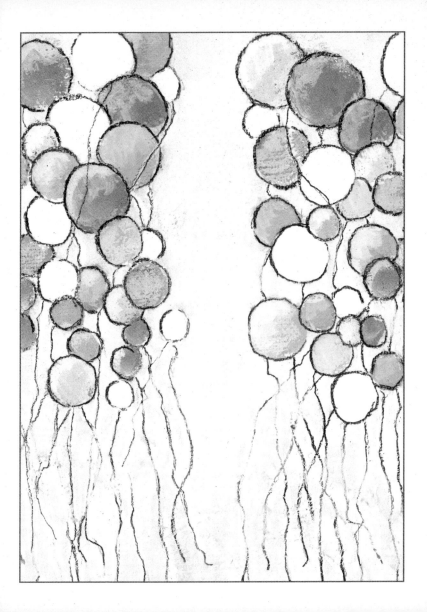

is a gift
only loaned to
us for a while.

And

someday

beyond

our

tears

and

all the

world's

wrongs...

beyond

the

clouds

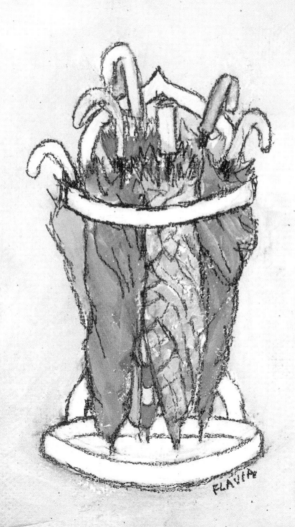

and all

we can see

and touch...

there

will be

love,

compassion

and

fairness...

and we

shall all

understand.

Flavia at work in her Santa Barbara studio

Flavia Weedn is a writer, painter and philosopher. Her life's work is about hope for the human spirit. "I want to reach people of all ages who have never been told, 'wait a minute, look around you. It's wonderful to be alive and every one of us matters. We can make a difference if we keep trying and never give up.'" It is Flavia's and her family's wish to awaken this spirit in each and every one of us. Flavia's messages are translated into many foreign languages on giftware, books and paper goods around the world.

To find out more about Flavia write to:
Weedn Studios, Ltd.
740 State Street, 3rd Floor
Santa Barbara, CA 93101 USA
or call: 805-564-6909